D1636441

# CROSSING STATE LINES

# CROSSING

# STATE LINES

## AN AMERICAN RENGA

EDITED BY BOB HOLMAN AND CAROL MUSKE-DUKES

FARRAR, STRAUS AND GIROUX    NEW YORK

Farrar, Straus and Giroux
18 West 18th Street, New York 10011

Distributed in Canada by D&M Publishers, Inc.
Printed in the United States of America
Published simultaneously in hardcover and paperback
First edition, 2011

Library of Congress Cataloging-in-Publication Data
Crossing state lines : an American renga / edited by Bob Holman and Carol
  Muske-Dukes. — 1st ed.
      p.   cm.
    ISBN 978-0-374-13213-2 (cloth : alk. paper) — ISBN 978-0-374-53274-1
(pbk. : alk. paper)
    1. United States—Poetry.   2. American poetry.   I. Holman, Bob, 1948–
II. Muske-Dukes, Carol, 1945–

PS595.U5C76 2011
811'.60835873

                                                            2010046559

Designed by Jonathan D. Lippincott

www.fsgbooks.com

10   9   8   7   6   5   4   3   2   1

Deep autumn—

my neighbor,

how does he live, I wonder?

—Bashō (translated by Robert Hass)

# INTRODUCTION

*Crossing State Lines: An American Renga* was born the dream of a dream and stands as a unique poem on the global landscape. It's an oxymoron, a "collaborative poem." It's a one-of-a-kind,[1] a fresh start, a spike. Yes, that's right, the orneriest of the arts[2] has decided to decamp for a fresh view of these states as seen by our poets, crisscrossing the country, following the seasons, having their say about politics and pastoral, and in general using words and words alone to make a journey into the revealing spirit.

How it came to be could not foretell what it came to be. The idea of fifty-four U.S. poets collaborating on a single poem represents the kind of audacious hope that is the whole project of America: Now and Here, the vision of a single artist who had never been involved in politics, now seizing a moment when the nation senses a new direction as a time to have art take its place in the national dialogue.

At least that's what I thought I heard Eric Fischl say, and it convinced me, utopic poet that I am. And my co-poet was to be Carol Muske-Dukes, who reckoned that what we were talk-

---

[1] Of course there's a tradition of collaborative poems: dadaist and surrealist literary games; certain works of the New York School, like John Ashbery and James Schuyler's novel, *A Nest of Ninnies*; the collection *Bean Spasms* by Ted Berrigan, Joe Brainard, and Ron Padget. The present volume is one of a kind in the sense that here poets are collaborating with poets they don't know, crossing genres and styles, and trusting the renga's form and purpose. (Does a poem have a purpose?)

[2] Dylan Thomas defined *his* poetry as "sullen."

ing about here was the Japanese "conversation" poem, the renga.

Carol and I have met a few times over the years, but just before signing on to this project we had what I would call an apocryphal event. This was at a party, a poets' party (but there were plenty of non-poets there too) at Howard Altmann's TriBeCa pad, the last of the salons. It was 'round midnight, the conversations had become music, and all of a sudden I found myself dueling with Ms. Muske-Dukes! (Not a place you want to be.) I have no idea how this came about, but the gist is simple enough—Carol was going on about Sylvia Plath, a poet whose work I admire, but I unfortunately mentioned that of the confessionalists I'd prefer to go with Anne Sexton. To say hell broke loose is an understatement, and the only conceivable way out was to have a Poetry Slam right then and there. So books were found, passed around, and Sylvia and Anne went head-to-head. It was a terrific match, with all present getting into the act. Long story short, Sylvia won the popular vote, but it was very close. I gained new respect for her, increased my love for Anne—and now understood what it was like to have an in-depth tête-à-tête with Ms. Muske-Dukes!

So, it was destined that Carol and I become collaborators, and I think you'll catch my intent here, which is that if the divine Ms. Muske-Dukes and I worked together on a project, then surely the rest of the United States' poetry community would join in. And while our goal of 100 percent participation by the entire population of the United States[3] was not quite met, those who did join in can fill volumes—and have.

---

[3] "We are all poets, really," as Walter Lowenfels proclaimed.

The poem moves, works, and, I hope, fulfills Fischl's vision. At the top, former poet laureate Robert Pinsky places us geographically and temporally: "Beginning of October, maples / kindle in the East, linked / to fire season in the West by what?" He continues with what connects us:

> Four time zones, oceans of prairies. Rocky
> precincts. Air, turbulence, icemelt. Ozone ranges . . .

and then concludes:

> What live or lethal or great or insane flows
> linking air to air? Or song to song?

What we have here in this poem are these links, poet to poet, across the land. "Live or lethal or great or insane" pretty much sums up the idea of this renga, its completed heave. And by the time that former poet laureate Robert Hass concludes, some 523 lines later, it's April and green, and we're having lunch staring out at the Pacific.

In between is the renga. Classically, in Japan, to create a renga a poet would write a haiku,[4] seventeen syllables in three lines (5-7-5, or so it's commonly done),[5] then pass to the next who would write another verse, a couplet of seven-syllable lines. This three plus two is then repeated, the poem passed along, the sake interceding (did I forget to mention the sake?—an integral

---

[4] Actually, the haiku evolved from the renga!

[5] Allen Ginsberg felt that equating a Chinese character and an English syllable was foolish at best, so prosaically adapted haiku to "American sentences": a single line of seventeen syllables: "Put on my tie in a taxi, short of breath, rushing to meditate."

part of renga parties/poetics) until, well, until the poem is over.[6] Although the Japanese have a name for the thirty-six liner—*kasen*—we decided early on against limiting ourselves to a kasen. In fact, we felt really expansive, and with the support of the staff of America: Now and Here, we used the "sky's not the limit" approach of organic "jes grew."[7]

A conversation. In the traditional renga, the conversation is between the poet and the preceding verse, in the manner laid out above. Because our communication was digital rather than physical, it was decided to give the rules some breath. So we asked for two five-line sequences from each poet, and while responding to what comes directly before was an option, the entire renga was thrown around the country like a lasso, a roller coaster, a jazz riff. And the poets could read the entire renga if they cared to.[8]

So you'll find them all herein, the amazing opening sequence, from Pinsky to Wright to Dove to Collins to Hammad to Muske-Dukes. There is plenty of news—we get a new president (via texting from Wheeler, also remarked on by Howe and Williams), who is gazelle-like when inaugurated (Waldman) and prayed for (Sanders). In fact, the prayer motif is developed by quite a few, until the renga itself becomes like a prayer for our country. Special days pass by: Halloween (Hirshfield), Day of the Dead (Harjo), Winter Solstice (Doty), New Year's (Lehman).

There's plenty of pastoral along the way: Billy Collins trans-

---

[6] "I never finished one yet."—Sekou Sundiata

[7] As in, the renga "jes grew"!

[8] Making a major difference from the surrealist "exquisite corpse," where the paper is folded and you're working off vibe and ether, able to see only part of what came before.

lates a pond (or is it the audience?) into "an asteroid" or "the flowers on the moon," flowers that are foreclosed in Suheir Hammad's following section. Ms. Muske-Dukes takes this metaphor deeper: while we pray that the house foreclosed on is not a home, she uses the ancient Chinese abacus to

> . . . add up what remains when
> What we thought was wealth is gone.

Kimiko Hahn slips into a tidal pool, where we find Charles Bernstein's No Exit sign and my own contribution's disappearing Tlingit.

And we drive a lot, too—Philip Levine gets us lost in Toledo; Edward Hirsch crosses state lines:

> Every state is a state of mind
>
> Every love is a drive
> toward a more perfect union

And Cleopatra Mathis steers us through a roadside attraction in Vermont—except somehow it's about recycling. And art.

Patricia Smith takes us to Chicago and an earful of blues, Adrienne Rich and Nicole Cooley stop off in New Orleans for music and mourning and loving.

David St. John, Jennifer Benka, Anne Waldman, and Edward Ledford, LTC, all take on the horror of war in general, as well as soldiers and their humanity. The themes weave and furl and haul back snippets and strike, and then Vijay Seshadri finds the big idea (politics in poetry):

Now at least we're out on the hillside
We can see it flashing up ahead, in the alder brakes.
Will we ever catch up to say how sorry we are?

As the poem lumbers, slinks, prowls and dances across the country, the varieties of poetry, the genres of contemporary poetics, clamber about like Lilliputians on the body politic.

Lisa Russ Spaar ("heir to hawthorn"), Susan Kinsolving ("a cumulus of time"), and Grace Schulman ("our native beech tree"), all find meaning through nature. For Carl Phillips, the poem is now a sea-falcon and is diving and "there's a cadence even / to brutality."

Michael Ryan makes a lightbulb joke that somehow turns into changing the president, and then Brenda Hillman picks up the joke at a café in Berkeley with a young couple in love. How does this happen? The renga has its own life and yet is still disobeying all rules (did everyone write ten lines? were they all four verses 3-2-3-2? I shan't spoil it! Read the poem to find out!). Rae Armantrout, like a contemporary Sappho, fragments a vignette with the chant "Sky god girl," a refrain picked up by Nicole Cooley.

Adrienne Rich creates a blues to the renga on the monitor while also packing in potato chips, Lehigh Valley, New Orleans (Katrina), and lesbianism, all in ten lines (she even includes a blues chorus!). She's followed by Jorie Graham, whose meditation on Emma Lazarus ("clenched hand—torch—give me / Your whom? your whom?— // Are we not what we invited in?") goes after the big picture, and gets there, in focus and yet elliptical, yakking about gas guzzlers while simultaneously lifting the poem to lyric. And then it's handed off to Donna Masini, whose objectivist-Creeley moment of reality in a Verizon store ("'There is no "them,"' he says") both completes and zings the prior verses. Masini leaves the section with "Christmas trees / . . . along the curb" (recycling), a theme picked up by Philip Schultz's ice skaters, only to have Luis J. Rodriguez take the season back out to California, where the windows are open "and the skating is done with rubber wheels."

An exegesis is not what this is about—it's an introduction, rather, a way of showing some of the connections in the renga. The excitement of those months when Stacy Hannah was sending out missives—where it is, where it's going, what it's becoming—can you feel that in the poem? Here's the iconic image, based on the *gestus* of American Sign Language poet Peter Cook: it's the Wild West, it's the Pony Express, delivering this luscious book into your hands, dear reader. And just as the poem journeyed all over these United States in its creation, so now the actual touring of the America: Now and Here project will bring the work back home—which is all over everywhere, along the road ongoing and the free spaces where the road is left behind. Deepest gratitude to the poets who made it happen, to Eric and Carol (!) and the ANH folks, and to the eternal poem that connects us all.

Bob Holman
The Bowery, October 18, 2009 / August 26, 2010

·

When Eric Fischl asked me to co-curate the poetry "wing" of the America: Now and Here union (with the inestimable Bob

Holman!), two truths became self-evident to me. One was that we needed to find a means to best display the expressive gifts of a substantial number of our extraordinary American poets—which would probably mean inventing our own state within the union of ANH. (No secession—but open borders!)

The other was that we required a forum in the form of a fluid document, a vessel that would somehow reflect a democratic vision of poetry (what Bob Holman rightly calls the "oxymoron" of the "collaborative" poem). We needed an approach to a famously solitary art and its practitioners—one that would link yet highlight individual voices.

I thought of the renga, the nine-hundred-year-old Japanese poem form (which means "linked poem") because a renga was/is a conversation, and it seemed the right time for America to hear its poets converse—perhaps in the style of the ancient practitioners. Renga participants would follow a set of game-like rules—and keep the poem flowing. Inspired by this choreography, contemporary poets would be given ten lines in which to say something of their own in response to the ten lines of the previous poet, working within the traditional syllabic form or not.

Bob and I (and Eric) came up with a title for our project—we decided (after much debate) on *Crossing State Lines: An American Renga*—and then we came up with a list of poets to invite to join the renga. Bob is famous for his spoken-word and performance-oriented poetry focus, a focus on orality, whereas I am a "page" poet, loyal to written words, to the enduring aesthetic, yet we quickly agreed on a list that included accomplished poets from differing backgrounds, ethnicities, styles, and rhetorics. Our collaboration (straining the metaphor a bit) was a happy example of the wholly intuitive yet plausibly democratic M.O.

Most poets whom we invited said yes immediately, others needed to imagine how they would fit in. Some said no, some remained unsure. We ended up with fifty-four poets who each rose to the challenge of the relay, accepting the word-torch as it was passed, then handing it on, keeping the flame high. We are well aware that there are many oversights, great poets we've missed—from Marilyn Nelson to Mark Strand to Terrance Hayes to Tom Healy and beyond—but the ongoingness of the renga gives us hope for future inclusiveness.

It was a dizzily fast turnaround—each poet only had about two days (tops) to come up with a response to the previous lines, to the accruing poem (except for former poet laureate Robert Pinsky, who set the poem going)—but the renga gradually became the Great American Renga, taking on its own power as it surged forward. Whitman would have dubbed it the "Body Electric"—but it is stop-time strophic, as each chorus voice is spotlit momentarily, in sequence.

The renga is bold, chiming, meditative, harmonic, dissonant, angry, surprising, lyrical, moving, ecstatic, and sorrowing. The renga poets talk about America: Now and Here—war, peace, the election of President Obama, the economy, foreclosure and family, bomb sites, battlegrounds, devastation and love, musical chords, and poetry itself. The poem starts out at the Atlantic and ends at the other edge of the continent, at the Pacific. There are stops in many different cities and states—and in the countries where America is at war. (One of the renga poets is an officer in the U.S. Army—Lt. Col. Edward Ledford, writing from Afghanistan.)

The renga is a historic poetic document like no other. It seems fair to say that there is nothing quite like it in literary history—or in collective imagination, perhaps because it *is* collective imagination—as it crosses state lines and states of mind.

Robert Pinsky notes "[f]our time zones, oceans of prairies." We cross the zones until we come to the edge, staring, with Robert Hass (and with Keats before him, "silent, upon a peak"), at where the Great American Renga has taken us, apart and together.

Carol Muske-Dukes
East Hampton, August 2010

# CROSSING STATE LINES

Beginning of October, maples
kindle in the East, linked
to fire season in the West by what?

Four time zones, oceans of prairies. Rocky
precincts. Air, turbulence, icemelt. Ozone ranges.

"Air held his breath" says Lincoln in
his poem. "Stealthily" at night
he "stole away"—to hear a madman singing.

What live or lethal or great or insane flows
linking air to air? Or song to song?

—ROBERT PINSKY

Not to meet a face
that did not seem to have a veil burned to its surface
which was only fog.

Standing up in the boat, the Seeker.
Stood on the landing rock, the Greeter.

In an unsung park where the river no longer drifts
an undistinguished pedestal says, Roger was
here. Now, dogs by day and drugs by dark.

A murder of crows, a short-tempered queue
of cars; this brilliant fence of gingko. This is Providence.

—C. D. WRIGHT

Shirtsleeved afternoons
turn toward leather as the trees
blush, scatter a last

few bright, weary wisps across
the great bruised heart of the South.

The spirit cup drifts
down the pond's moon-sparked highway.
Far laughter, shadows.

Love or poison? Your turn. Drink
to the star-drenched latitudes!

—RITA DOVE

A few of those rings
that run around the spun earth
cross this southern state.

Is that what the frogs discuss
in the dark beyond the pool

light's blue-green shimmer
or is it a more ancient
topic that stirs them?

an asteroid they noticed
or the flowers on the moon.

—BILLY COLLINS

a field of foreclosed flowers
dreams of living rooms
glass ware china ware nowhere

the beautiful struggle here
pray a house is not a home

the middle of october
leaves carry the sun
families furnish rentals

the margins gather for warmth
where the buffalo don't roam

—SUHEIR HAMMAD

Pray a house is not
A home. And while you're at it,
Pray that prayer is

Not a funhouse mirror slid
Between terror and God's face.

Time to make something
From nothing—garden, star chart,
Beehive, birdhouse, abacus

To add up what remains when
What we thought was wealth is gone.

—CAROL MUSKE-DUKES

Season named by what
is no longer, having left
the garden gate just

open enough for the goats
to wander in, to rip out

any trace of green
as if all along they knew
while city trains pass

with men who stare into news
papers meant to understand.

—SOPHIE CABOT BLACK

The eyes, splendid in
a bowl of moon, & the tragic
head served on a silver

tray—I understood fate most
as a boy at the Rodin:

each his own marble
bust, light-stricken guards, & open
gallery. Of course!

Parades of Ugolinos,
chewing in bloodsucking silence.

—MAJOR JACKSON

Outside, on blighted branches,
tomatoes' orange lanterns. Paradise, too, is hell-lit.
Soon now, Day of the Dead—

Heaped platters hauled to the vanished.
Graveside feasting dusted with sugar at midnight.

Take the highway south then.
Whitman's abattoir fills the nostrils along I-5.
Just past it, blossoming citrus.

The late moon flenses cows to meat and marble.
We drive on at the speed of prayer.

—JANE HIRSHFIELD

Tonight the dead dance.
Feed the dancers sweets, flowers.
Pray to nourish rain.

Scrape clean graves of our lush debts:
Butts, foil, diapers, tears. We're done.

Moon lighting up sky
At night, over black mesa.
No buffalo bones.

We'll all make it home somehow,
When the dance is over. Rain.

—JOY HARJO

And the sky that sends it down
was once, in 1933,
the bowl

for dust the wind reamed clean the
silos with. Its rain, now, spills

a bank, slaps beads against
the flank of an old shed.
         Within, wet, a girl

thumbs nu prez xtc ryt?—
SEND. She hardly hears the wind.

Those years of our hurt
Brokered by the war's despair
Became flags of art

Waving in November air
The simple songs of the heart

Arise as we start
Over knowing we might dare
Now the grieving part

For those whose lives stood apart
Too long in the bloody cut

—DAVID ST. JOHN

And then it happened—a shifting so accumulated

that it tipped—like a ball shivering on the rim

tapped over—into the basket.

And we were cheering, incredulous,

some of us standing up from where we'd been sitting,

standing up in front of our televisions,

some weeping in public, or kissing someone, or

still standing, dumb and smiling,

as what we had asked for walked out on the stage, grave

and graceful—and we looked and looked at the man.

—MARIE HOWE

Corrupt unscrupulous treacherous
opprobrious traitorous felonious lawless
ignoble sinister atrocious foul
demonic malignant immoral disgraceful

—Then, at the distance of dawn, glow
A distant lucent hint of glow

Arrogant evil iniquitous odious base
reprehensible wicked villainous vile
pernicious venomous criminal shameful
unforgivable unforgiven never forgiven

—Then a crystalline autumn apple of air
and we breathed breathed again breathed

—C. K. WILLIAMS

ahh unh ahh unh ahh
with lets for the braces and
halters for losses

the iron lung hastened the
fastening process

—HEATHER McHUGH

After he goes on about hell, she says
"We in heaven." No, Leo says—he's driving—
"We dead or that's Toledo up ahead."

No more dead than yesterday, no more
alive, either, just about the same.

You drive all night to get somewhere
you've never been only to wind up
nowhere or if you keep going some place

worse, if there is a worse. Or—if Leo
is right—holy Toledo! And we been there.

—PHILIP LEVINE

The trees lined up along the roads
that veined out in different directions
sometimes divided sometimes united

The fall air bordered on winter

How many state lines did we cross
as we drove across a wide country
sometimes divided sometimes united

Every state is a state of mind

Every love is a drive
toward a more perfect union

—EDWARD HIRSCH

And in Vermont—up a twisting hill
the Barrel Man's sign: twenty-five-foot
collage of barrels hooked and joined

to make a man. 10 bucks apiece, he says—
Soap can, oilcan, what-have-you can
to fill with salt and sand, dented metal

presiding over ice grip, sleet to snow.
Each wood-slat throne adorned
with rusty shovel, each can a turquoise

charm against the car's careening!

—CLEOPATRA MATHIS

Sagittal, the geese, like a dismantled dormer,
a gable of hearts. How instinctively they go.

I know the tidal blue mountains
shifting at dawn beneath their passage

over philandering clouds more true to life
than any vow. Though I'm heir to hawthorn,

nandina, holly, puritan barb, reserve & blood—
my pounding ribcage follows them,

pulled into air in knell of chthonic joy
only the hidden, then harvested can know.

—LISA RUSS SPAAR

A cumulus of time drifts
over snow, petals, papers, ash.
We sleep

and spin, synapse as solstice
shortened days, lengthened light.

Clouds and continents
immediacy and history
become one.

The old man's face wanes, ardent
despite the distance and dark.

—SUSAN KINSOLVING

Love stays
and that's American.
Look! Our native beech tree,

short on green this winter,
won't shed withered leaves.

Scraps cling to boughs,
strawlike but amber in sun
as wind ruffles them.

The crackling you hear
is only deep breathing.

—GRACE SCHULMAN

How many poets does it take to change
a lightbulb? Two. One to change
the lightbulb and one to

envy the one that got
to change the lightbulb.

How many poets does it take to change a lightbulb?
Two. One to change the lightbulb
and one to write, "I'm screwed."

How many poets does it take to change
a country? How many presidents? How much pain?

—MICHAEL RYAN

—& a lightbulb turns
earth. Berkeley lovers in a
Thai café: mint, sweet

basil. Geminid showers
all this week . . . Solstice, almost—

You can take money
out of the empire but you
can't take the empire—

Look. Enough of these wars. A
rabbit crouches in the moon—

—BRENDA HILLMAN

In front of the craft shop,
a small nativity,
mother, baby, sheep
made of blue
and white balloons.

\*

Sky
     god
         girl.

Pick out the one
that doesn't belong.

—RAE ARMANTROUT

Girl God Sky: at the levee's
edge, she waits, a stick in the dirt.

Towns still stuck at the Gulf's edge:
Pascagoula, Waveland. Miles

of highway. An empty trench.
Flooded. Now unflooded. Gone.

She lies on mud and leaves,
tries not to disappear.

—NICOLE COOLEY

Rising wild onion sun painting the Illinois prairie.
A wind dances on buffalo eyes—horns, beards, winter fur.
Herd breathes vapor, turns, mists away.

Handful of dung and corn seed slammed into the ground.
With spit, with blood, it grows, as eyes shrink, ribs, body,

Skeletal collapse. It grows, spreading corn wildfire—
Corn running, silk scarf, pumping heart,
Indian body, just bones. Indian opens an eye—

Sprinting trees can't catch up, sun circles behind,
Kernels pop off. Rockies rise. He leaps up, gone!

—PETER COOK

Old leaves, deer tracks in the mud around the front porch,
step-chart for a crazy dance. Just past the solstice and out here
at land's end the song to song is blue jay blustering rivals,

three-note chickadee saying what? _____ __ __. Cuneiform,
I read, was the same physical work as texting, quick

little pushes on clay instead of the iPhone screen. Message to
        song,
then to now; the days shifting longer, possibility rising,
this year . . . While far off, in the capital, some idiots are
        chased away,

and others invited to the stage. How much to hope?
[portion of line missing—tablet cracked] Birdsong, ascendant
        notes.

—MARK DOTY

Maybe you've seen how a sea-falcon,
hovering above its own reflection,
will at last strike through it to the silver
life flashing just beneath it, and thus
survive. How there's a cadence even

to brutality. As it turns out, there were
always choices. Sing, or don't sing.
Ritual, and the unraveling of it. You
all over again, but bearing the light
for once steadily forward, as if for us both.

—CARL PHILLIPS

The snow is expected. It's the day before
The day before and snow is expected
Across the lake. The story doesn't end
Though the year does. The snow resumes.

I liked the present better when it was still
The future, like a kid who wanted a chemistry set
For his birthday, because the flasks and beakers
Were beautiful, full of the warm south.

And there you have it: sun's bravery, wind's power
Shaking the powder out of the spruces and pines.

—DAVID LEHMAN

Renga, renga on the screen where has all the music gone?
State Line potato chips, wish I had a few in hand

Down in the Lehigh Valley at the bottom of the bottomless
        ditch
Lived alone in a cabin attending the railway switch

Went down to St. James Infirmary, saw my baby there
Bees and butterflies pickin out her eyes
On the streets of New Orleans

You know I'm a crawlin kingsnake baby and I rules my den

Women loving each other, they don't think about no man
They ain't playing it secret no more. These women playing a
        wide open hand

But actually nothing's—nothing's—gone, and nothing's new
About this new slim chip of time we've just now crossed the
        border of,
Adding one atomic second to the flowering

Open-handed clock—feel it?—we've not been here
Before we think but the price of gas is down again and the sale

Of guzzlers up—oh brother—land
Is not our land—I pull the last leeks up from under
Frost and point the round white-haired root-ends straight up

To the invisible day moon, full moon—clenched hand—
        torch—give me
Your whom? your whom?—

Are we not what we invited in?

—JORIE GRAHAM

"We're not them,"
the man at Verizon
Help Desk says.

"OK," I say, "who is 'them'?"
"There is no 'them,' " he says.

Epiphany. A sign
outside Prince Realty:
Need Help? Inquire Within.

All the dry stiff Christmas trees
tip to trunk along the curb.

—DONNA MASINI

The same sad spark inhales itself
all the way to its beginning.
Man wants to be happy,

cannot help wanting to be
happy, Pascal sighs, blithely.

I'm trying to be. We all are.
Spinach is, cucumbers extremely so.
It's winter, again,

Oh hum, the river freezes at night.
Ah, the pretty kids, skating!

—PHILIP SCHULTZ

rivers freeze in the east, but in California the sun-baked homes
yawn with open windows and the skating is done with rubber
        wheels

it's winter still, but we're not on the same terrain, or under the
        same
blessed eye, or lacking of spinach and other green things

you curse, we laugh, but then fires explode and consume with
        winds
that possibly tickled your nose one day—somehow none of us
        are immune

disasters are our lot, sun-blistered face or frozen smile—it's
        more about
whatever wholeness we hang on to when nature and our
        natures break

and what language of that memory can elevate us to try again
we've been here before, and we have to save the world every
        time

—LUIS J. RODRIGUEZ

Magma, negative ions, heady politics
Continental Divide's a way to crack your heart
One eye on the Pacific, other gazes east

Up there in Washington, D.C., where they run your life from
It's celestial now, 44th Prez gorgeous as a gazelle, & smart too
     hooray

May he not be a warring one, close torture & all its
     accoutrements
Ancient bristlescones awaken in beauty of astonishment
January crisp inauguration eve has a dream

Gay civil rights still waiting in the wings show's on
Citizens (all together now) reach out to the Middle East

—ANNE WALDMAN

What's the big idea? And then again
what idea was so big it couldn't come through
the little door. It waited outside for us,

throwing pebbles at the window.
Finally it gave up and went away.

Now at least we're out on the hillside
We can see it flashing up ahead, in the alder brakes.
Will we ever catch up to say how sorry we are?

Believer and nonbeliever, each on the hillside,
each wondering if the other is right.

—VIJAY SESHADRI

Five, six—and righteous,
the child in green in Gaza
stands in her wrecked home,

grubby, indignant. Her hands
point; she explains what was done

bombed, burned. It smells like
gas. We had to throw our clothes
away! The earrings my

father gave me! No martyr,
resistant. The burnt cradle . . .

—MARILYN HACKER

*Oud*, *ney*, *riqq*, *kanun*
artillery in moonlight
music in Gaza.

From the cold echo chamber
a siren's long melody.

Neon-tinted snow
parking lot slash dressing room
dobro, pedal steel

Fingering the fretted neck
G, F sharp, B, C sharp, A.

—PAUL SIMON

If there is a God,
Please may He or She
Assist our new President

Guide him to Peace and Service
Help calm the Military

Grant prosperity to every
Last human on
Broad-breasted Earth

The semi-bliss of Nat'l Health
And a Sharing of the Wealth

—EDWARD SANDERS

"No Images" would be perfect
for this renga snow,
chill in the cut.

Air rocks
Oppenheimer clouds.

Swear to God, word,
if Doña Maria loses
her botanica—

Vapor, flakes,
crystal, kaboom . . .

—WILLIE PERDOMO

Whoa! Hold on there, Partner! Time for you
To speak up. This here Renga's a verbal democracy—
Bambara, Hopi, Español. I hanker to hear

Your voice cross lines like sunrise from Denver
To Kansas City, chasing the groundhog home to spring.

Mother of All Tongues, whoop-ti-do!
English, Nuyoriqueño, Frisian, lingual whoosharooni,
Carny barker barks—slippy slang, Wu-Tang Clan,

Tlingit, Maori, Mayan. Poems are made of words.
Pass it on. You talkin' to me? Do tell! I'm all ears.

—BOB HOLMAN

The "flow of the wind,"
"wind elegance," "wind madness":
renga's mother stock.

Or motherboard, the logic
open-sourced, a free-for-all.

Only disconnect—
if the circle were perfect
it would be a noose—

let me mention the season.
Downpour tips my cup of gold.

—DANA GOODYEAR

The February
moon, its arms around itself,
still sits stalled beneath

points being made about love
and death in the sky above.

The moral is spread
on some month-old snow out back—
a design we like

to think night can make of day,
the summons again delayed.

—J. D. McCLATCHY

I pray to be anointed
by a bluesman's spittle.
His roar began

when the jukebox stopped taking
quarters. He knows my city

in his throat—
Chicago, he growls,
checking my skin for signs of fever.

I burn concrete, El train, the
Alabama I don't know.

—PATRICIA SMITH

*As if* you could fight fire with ire

or tame thought with torn

disclosures.

*Fear* gnaws, money

down drain, spent in vain,

foreclosures

*Sure*, or just paddle out the back way

behind the No Exit sign, barely clutching your nearly

foregone

enclosures.

—CHARLES BERNSTEIN

the people are ready
to record the confession

how a body is the same
as a rock in red radar

how computers lock
a missile on a target

what it feels like to finger
the key the trigger

the look of lips
saying sorry

—JENNIFER BENKA

Love the tidal pool!
the microscopic wiggle
of the horseshoe crab

Shedding and shedding till
the body triggers Exit Sign!

Shells are cool to shed.
Not so—the Ozone Layer,
kindness, Tlingit, say—

—KIMIKO HAHN

So much talk beyond ourselves.
If our shells could only speak

More of the nothingness.
Oceans without you.
Puddles made of us.

Maybe, the slag ash we drank
Affected our brains—or maybe

We swam too far from knowing
Where the shore meets
The edge of nowhere—maybe.

—MARC KELLY SMITH

Oceans of prairies, black mesa and buffalo bones, the great
        bruised heart of the South,
or down in the Lehigh Valley at the bottom of the bottomless
        ditch,
carny barker barks, a bluesman's spittle, Ugolinos chewing in
        bloodsucking silence, dogs by day and drugs by dark,
Berkeley lovers in a Thai café, praying for prayer, or what night
        can make of day,
sparrows churring above rockweed, eelgrass, glasswort in
        Orient, as we gaze eastward across the tidal wetlands
        and then the sea,

all hurrying forwards, towards who we'll become, one way
        only, one life only: free in time but not from it,
here in the country the living make together, make & unmake
        over & over—
Quick, quick, ask heaven of it, of every mortal relation, feeling
        that is fleeing,
for what would the heart be without a heaven to set it on?
I can't help thinking no word will ever be as full of life as this
        world, I can't help thinking of thanks.

—SUJI KWOCK KIM

"thanks," replied the hurricane/tornado.

try 'n' place my crazy song now.
isolated. an image. afterthought to the sequence.

lo, civilization is a joke to me, always helping.
conviction lacking account.

oklahoma is a burst metaphor for formulaic forgetting.

prayer dust on the minds of advanced fixers
standing behind the glass.

the uncomfortable wreckage is at 190-ludicrous-figure-
continuing mph.

tantrum heading in the direction of definitions.

—BEAU SIA

Let's say physicists
know what they're talking about.
Everywhere's a cen-

ter—the universe spreads out
from its first tiny birth-spark.

Yet, in Ohio,
along one stagnant farm pond,
a great blue heron

steps from splash to splash, and thus
shortens the distance to you.

—DAVID BAKER

A dark mood so absorbs the afternoon
That dry wind flakes the edges of the earth
And despair encapsulates experience.

Mind breaks loose to cut through time and space
Beyond the pounding surf, the dark cloud-banks
Reflected in the craggy ocean's depth.

The poem that approximates the mind's path
Probes the multi-layered mysteries, explores
Those crevices that thought has seldom touched,

And ends where it began: so never ends.

—WILLIAM JAY SMITH

Pathogens injected Trojan-horse-style; temple walls crumble
        before a small
lexicon, altared and stable, unsullied, too briefly a miracle. Our

neo-tragedy was their crazy carte blanche.
You'd think they'd have read their Homer. But, like

slapping the moron beside the bully, we invade Babylon to
applause, which muted, *a-hem*, throats cleared for political
        posterity.

Soldiers are nothing more than pharmakon charged with the
        damned's duty,
enlisted to oaths that only finally matter when we wish they
        didn't. The

soldier-philosopher turns the gun on himself to salvage some
        meaning.
A smirk and crooked smile, *Heh heh heh, sure showd em, didn
        we, Dead-eye.*

—EDWARD LEDFORD, LTC, U.S. ARMY

Oh well along the coast in greeny April
Forgiveness is the blue sheen
Of lupine on a windy hillside,

The grasses stating their case for
and against "the continent's violent requiem."

The year turning as a renga turns
Toward its source, rivery, many-voiced,,
But what source, really, in the turning?

So the hikers who have walked to the cliff's edge
Unpack their lunches and stare at the Pacific.

—ROBERT HASS

# ABOUT THE CONTRIBUTORS, IN THEIR OWN WORDS

RAE ARMANTROUT's book *Versed* won the 2010 Pulitzer Prize for poetry. *Money Shot* will be published by Wesleyan in early 2011.

DAVID BAKER has lived in the rural Midwest most of his life. He is poetry editor of *The Kenyon Review*.

JENNIFER BENKA worked for homeless and women's advocacy organizations before landing in New York City and at Poets & Writers, where she worked as the managing director for close to a decade.

CHARLES BERNSTEIN, Nowhereville; excommunicate, First Church, Poetic License; Director, Center for Avant-Garde Comedy & Stand-Up Poetry.

SOPHIE CABOT BLACK, Fairfield County, Connecticut; small farmer in hedge country; also teaches at Columbia University.

BILLY COLLINS, New York and Florida; was U.S. poet laureate (2001–2003). His latest collection is *Horoscopes for the Dead*.

PETER COOK, Chicago; creates/performs his American Sign Language poems with Kenny Lerner as part of Flying Words.

NICOLE COOLEY grew up in New Orleans. Her latest book is *Breach*, a collection of poems about Hurricane Katrina and the Gulf Cost.

MARK DOTY, New York City and East Hampton; teaches at Rutgers University; latest book: *Fire to Fire: New and Selected Poems*.

RITA DOVE, born and reared in Akron, Ohio; is Commonwealth Professor of English at the University of Virginia, and is a Pultizer Prize winner and former U.S. poet laureate.

DANA GOODYEAR, Los Angeles; writes for *The New Yorker* and teaches literary nonfiction at the University of Southern California.

JORIE GRAHAM was raised in Italy. She now divides her time between Cambridge, where she teaches at Harvard, and Normandy, France.

MARILYN HACKER, Paris, France. This renga led to a collaboration with the Palestinian-American poet Deema Shehabi, now some seventy renga long.

KIMIKO HAHN, Brooklyn and Mattituck, New York; teaches at Queens College/CUNY; latest books are *The Narrow Road to the Interior* and *Toxic Flora.*

SUHEIR HAMMAD's books include *breaking poems* and *born palestinian, born black.*

JOY HARJO, Albuquerque—Honolulu—Oklahoma; poet, musician, playwright, and performer, and at work on the musical *I Think I Love You, An All Night Round Dance.*

ROBERT HASS grew up and writes in and around the San Francisco Bay Area. He has seven grandchildren, four of whom are girls, and he sometimes writes and translates poems.

BRENDA HILLMAN, a native of Tucson, Arizona; is the Olivia Filippi Professor of Poetry at Saint Mary's College in Moraga, California, and works with CodePink, a women-initiated social justice group.

EDWARD HIRSCH, Chicago, the heartland; is president of the John Simon Guggenheim Memorial Foundation, New York.

JANE HIRSHFIELD, a poet, essayist, and translator with ten

published books, lives in the San Francisco Bay Area, on the hem of Mount Tamalpais.

BOB HOLMAN is from Kentucky and is a native New Yorker living on the Bowery. He's the founder of the Bowery Poetry Club, teaches at NYU and Columbia, and is codirector of the Endangered Language Alliance. (Coeditor with Carol Muske-Dukes of *Crossing State Lines*.)

MARIE HOWE was raised in Rochester, New York, and lives in and writes from New York City.

MAJOR JACKSON, Burlington, Vermont; is an aspiring sommelier and a professor of English at the University of Vermont.

SUJI KWOCK KIM, Cambridge, Massachusetts, and Milton, New York; is author of *Notes from the Divided Country* and a professor at UMass-Boston.

SUSAN KINSOLVING's fourth book of poems is *My Glass Eye*. As a librettist, her operatic works have been performed in New York, California, and Italy.

EDWARD LEDFORD is a lieutenant colonel in the United States Army, currently serving in Kabul, Afghanistan. He received his B.A. in English from the Virginia Military Institute in 1987 and his M.A. in English from the University of Alabama in 1995, and will attend the University of Virginia School of Law in 2011, after retiring from the army. Ed is a native of Asheville, North Carolina, making his home in Charlottesville.

DAVID LEHMAN lives in New York City but wrote his renga lines in Ithaca, New York, where he spends summers and some winter weeks.

PHILIP LEVINE gave up Detroit for Fresno, Fresno for Barcelona, Barcelona for Brooklyn, and now has all three.

DONNA MASINI is a poet and novelist, lives in New York City, and is a professor of English and creative writing at Hunter College.

CLEOPATRA MATHIS, Vermont; is a professor of English at Dartmouth College, and has published six books of poems.

J. D. MCCLATCHY lives on the Connecticut coastline, teaches at Yale, and has published six books of poems, and his libretti are performed in opera houses around the world.

HEATHER MCHUGH was born in San Diego, was raised in southern Virginia, was educated in New England (housed in Maine for decades), and finally settled in Seattle—pretty much covering the four quadrants of the country.

CAROL MUSKE-DUKES (born in St. Paul, Minnesota; New York, Louisiana) was appointed poety laureate of California in 2008. Professor at USC; eighth book of poems, *Twin Cities*, forthcoming. (Coeditor with Bob Holman of *Crossing State Lines*.)

WILLIE PERDOMO is the author of *Where a Nickel Costs a Dime* and *Smoking Lovely*. He lives in New York City.

CARL PHILLIPS was born in Everett, Washington, calls Cape Cod home, and teaches in St. Louis.

ROBERT PINSKY has performed his poems with jazz musicians including Vijay Iyer and Stan Strickland.

ADRIENNE RICH: I was born and raised in Baltimore, Maryland. Have lived in New York, Massachusetts, and Vermont; since 1984 in California. The lines I used come from blues and folk poetry, a neglected source of music and sensibility in America here and now.

LUIS J. RODRIGUEZ, Los Angeles; is founder/editor of Tia Chucha Press and cofounder of Tia Chucha's Centro Cultural and Bookstore.

MICHAEL RYAN writes poems and essays and teaches at the University of California, Irvine.

EDWARD SANDERS, known as founder of the Investigative Poetry movement, was born in Kansas City and has been writing and living in Woodstock, New York, for thirty-six years.

GRACE SCHULMAN, whose most recent collection of poems is *The Broken String*, is a native New Yorker who lives part of the time in Long Island's East End.

PHILIP SCHULTZ, East Hampton; won the Pulitzer Prize in 2008, and is the founder/director of the Writers Studio.

VIJAY SESHADRI writes poetry and teaches prose in and around New York City.

BEAU SIA is from Oklahoma City. He loves to play, but does not play around.

PAUL SIMON lives in Connecticut and is a songwriter and singer.

MARC KELLY SMITH is the Grand Slampapi of the International Poetry Slam movement. Say "So what?" to that.

PATRICIA SMITH is the author of *Blood Dazzler*, a finalist for the National Book Award, and is a professor of creative writing at the City University of New York.

WILLIAM JAY SMITH, Cummington, Massachusetts; will publish in 2011 *My Friend Tom: The Poet-Playwright Tennessee Williams*.

LISA RUSS SPAAR was born and raised in (sub)urban New Jersey, although she's lived most of her life in relatively pastoral settings below the Mason-Dixon Line.

DAVID ST. JOHN was once introduced by Charles Wright as "the Mallarmé of Venice Beach."

ANNE WALDMAN is the cofounder of the Jack Kerouac School

of Disembodied Poetics and the author of *Manatee/ Humanity* and *The Iovis Trilogy: Colors in the Mechanism of Concealment*.

SUSAN WHEELER, East Millstone, New Jersey; teaches at Princeton University.

C. K. WILLIAMS's most recent books are *Wait*, poems; *On Whitman*, a study; and *A Not Scary Story About Big Scary Things*, a story for children.

C. D. WRIGHT lives outside of Providence, Rhode Island. Her new book is *One with Others: A Little Book of Her Days*.

# AMERICA: NOW AND HERE

> The idea is simple. Let's explore a theme that everybody shares and build a dialogue around it: **America**. We'll start by sharing our ideas and experiences through the art that we make. Now, it's your turn. Let's use art to have a dialogue about **America**.                    —Eric Fischl

America: Now and Here is a cross-country journey of art and ideas. Conceived of by the artist Eric Fischl, it is bringing art and artists (including visual artists, musicians, poets, playwrights, and filmmakers) to large and small communities across America to ignite creativity, to launch thoughtful dialogue, and to inspire a bold vision for our shared future.

Visit our website at www.americanowandhere.org.